REMARKABLE
PEOPLE

Johnny Depp

by Anita Yasuda

www.av2books.com

AV² provides enriched content that supplements and complements this book. Weigl's AV² books strive to create inspired learning and engage young minds in a total learning experience.

Your AV² Media Enhanced books come alive with...

Audio
Listen to sections of the book read aloud.

Key Words
Study vocabulary, and complete a matching word activity.

Video
Watch informative video clips.

Quizzes
Test your knowledge.

Embedded Weblinks
Gain additional information for research.

Slide Show
View images and captions, and prepare a presentation.

Try This!
Complete activities and hands-on experiments.

... and much, much more!

Go to **www.av2books.com**, and enter this book's unique code.

BOOK CODE

J527750

AV² **by Weigl** brings you media enhanced books that support active learning.

Published by AV² by Weigl
350 5th Avenue, 59th Floor
New York, NY 10118

www.av2books.com   www.weigl.com

Library of Congress Cataloging-in-Publication Data

Yasuda, Anita.
  Johnny Depp / Anita Yasuda.
      p. cm. -- (Remarkable people)
Includes index.
ISBN 978-1-61913-536-9 (hardcover : alk. paper) -- ISBN 978-1-61913-591-8 (softcover : alk. paper)
1. Depp, Johnny--Juvenile literature. 2. Motion picture actors and actresses--United States--Biography--Juvenile literature. I. Title.
PN2287.D47Y37 2013
791.4302'8092--dc23
[B]
                                        2012000949

Printed in the United States of America in North Mankato, Minnesota
1 2 3 4 5 6 7 8 9 0 16 15 14 13 12

WEP170512
062012

Editor: Heather Kissock
Design: Terry Paulhus

Photograph Credits
Weigl acknowledges Getty Images as the primary image supplier for this title. Every reasonable effort has been made to trace ownership and to obtain permission to reprint copyright material. The publishers would be pleased to have any errors or omissions brought to their attention so that they may be corrected in subsequent printings.

Contents

Who Is Johnny Depp?

Johnny Depp is one of the world's best-known movie stars. He has won several awards for his acting and has been **nominated** for three **Academy Awards**. Johnny has made a career out of portraying quirky characters. His choice of roles in films such as *Edward Scissorhands*, *Alice in Wonderland*, *Charlie and the Chocolate Factory*, and the voice behind **animated** features such as *Rango* keeps fans interested. Johnny loves the process of acting but is not comfortable seeing himself on screen. He has seen only a few of his own movies.

> *"I am doing things that are true to me. The only thing I have a problem with is being labeled."*

Johnny enjoys spending time with his family and friends when he is not filming. He is an active father who can be seen taking his two children to concerts and other events. As a part-time musician, he sometimes joins other artists on stage to play a **set** or two.

Growing Up

John Christopher Depp II was born on June 9, 1963, in Owensboro, Kentucky. His parents moved to Miramar, Florida, when he was seven. This was one of many moves for Johnny. By the time he was in his mid-teens, the family had moved more than 20 times.

Johnny's father, John Christopher, was a **civil engineer**. His mother, Elizabeth "Betty" Sue, worked as a waitress in local diners. After his parents divorced, Johnny continued to live with his mother, his sister Christie, and his brother Danny. Johnny's other sister, Debbie, went to live with their father.

Johnny began playing guitar at the age of 12. He and a couple of friends formed a band called The Kids. They began playing at backyard parties and clubs. When Johnny was 20, he married makeup artist Lori Allison. The couple moved to Los Angeles with the other members of The Kids hoping to get the band a **recording contract**.

■ Johnny's parents remain an important part of his life. In 1999, they watched Johnny receive a star on the Hollywood Walk of Fame.

Get to Know Kentucky

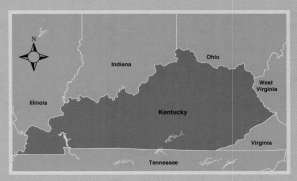

FLOWER
Goldenrod

TREE
Tulip Poplar

BIRD
Cardinal

The world's longest cave is located in Kentucky. Mammoth Cave is the second oldest tourist attraction in the United States, after Niagara Falls.

Frankfort is the capital city of Kentucky.

The state motto of Kentucky is "United We Stand, Divided We Fall."

The Kentucky Derby is one of the oldest Thoroughbred horse races in the United States. It is held each May at Churchill Downs.

Due to his father's career, Johnny Depp moved from place to place as a child. What impact do you think moving around had on Johnny? Do you think it helped him become an actor? How? How many times have you moved in your life? What do you like about moving to a new place? What do you dislike? Why do you think you feel this way?

Practice Makes Perfect

In Los Angeles, Johnny and his band worked as **opening acts** for other bands. They earned little to no money for these performances, so Johnny and his bandmates had to find other jobs. Johnny worked as a **telemarketer** selling ballpoint pens. He made about $50 a week.

Johnny's luck changed when he met actor Nicolas Cage. Nic told Johnny that he should try to get an acting job. Johnny went to see Nic's agent, who soon found work for the **novice** actor. After working as an **extra** in several movies, Johnny's first acting job was in the horror movie *A Nightmare on Elm Street*. Johnny played the role of Glen. Glen is just one of the many characters who dies at the hands of the movie's villain, Freddy Krueger.

Johnny has often credited Nicolas Cage with getting him started as an actor.

Encouraged by his early success, Johnny began taking acting lessons at The Loft Studio in Los Angeles. Soon after, director Oliver Stone cast Johnny in *Platoon* as a Vietnamese-speaking interpreter. Oliver pushed Johnny to give his best performance in every scene. The experience made Johnny want to be a better actor.

In 1987, Johnny was offered a role as an undercover cop on the television show *21 Jump Street*. Almost overnight, he became a teen idol, receiving 10,000 fan letters a month. Johnny found the show to be a great learning experience, but he did not like being on it. He left the show after four years.

In 1990, Johnny starred in the movie *Cry-Baby*. This movie was a spoof on 1950s teen movies.

Key Events

With an eye to moving away from his teen idol status, Johnny took a role in director Tim Burton's *Edward Scissorhands*. He played Edward, a man who had scissors instead of hands. Johnny received good reviews for his sensitive portrayal of Edward. Johnny related to Edward as he, too, had never felt he fit in with his peers. In 1991, Johnny received a **Golden Globe** nomination for *Edward Scissorhands*.

Throughout the 1990s, Johnny worked steadily, portraying a string of unusual characters in movies such as *What's Eating Gilbert Grape?* and *Benny & Joon*. He earned a reputation for taking on challenging and diverse roles. In *Sleepy Hollow*, for instance, he played the role of awkward schoolteacher Ichabod Crane. In *Chocolat*, which was released in 2000, he portrayed the romantic **leading man**. *Chocolat* was later nominated for five Academy Awards.

In 2003, Johnny played the role of Captain Jack Sparrow in *Pirates of the Caribbean: The Curse of the Black Pearl*. The movie was a **blockbuster** success. Johnny received his first Academy Award nomination for his portrayal of Jack Sparrow.

■ Captain Jack Sparrow was a supporting character in the first *Pirates of the Caribbean* movie. Johnny's performance received so much attention that Sparrow became the lead character in the sequels.

Thoughts from Johnny

Johnny is grateful for the life his career has given him. Here are some of his thoughts on acting, fame, and life in general.

Johnny explains what actors bring to a role.

"With any part you play, there is a certain amount of yourself in it. There has to be, otherwise it's just not acting."

Johnny talks about moving all the time as a child.

"I was all over the place and always the new kid at school, which is never easy."

Johnny talks about what he hopes to achieve as an actor.

"If there's any message to my work, it is ultimately that it's OK to be different, that it's good to be different, that we should question ourselves before we pass judgment on someone who looks different, behaves different, talks different, is a different color."

Johnny explains why he chooses certain roles.

"People say I make strange choices, but they're not strange for me. ...I'm fascinated by human behavior, by what's underneath the surface, by the worlds inside people."

Johnny discusses his feelings toward being a celebrity.

"Outside in life people are looking and staring at you. You see them taking your picture all the time with their iPhones. You become a kind of novelty in the world."

Johnny talks about how being a successful actor has changed his life.

"I do realize and understand very well on a profound level how lucky I am and what a privileged position it is and what it's done ultimately for me, my family and my kids."

What Is an Actor?

Actors use speech, body language, or movement to pretend to be other people, or characters. The stage, radio, television, and movies all provide opportunities for actors to perform. Often, actors must learn lines and movements that are written in **scripts**. Sometimes, actors do not use a script. This is called improvisation.

In order to play different roles, actors need talent and experience. Usually, actors train at acting schools or work with an acting coach to improve their skills. They take classes in voice and **diction**.

Some actors, such as Johnny Depp, have other talents. Johnny has used his musical skills in several roles. In the movie *Cry-Baby*, Johnny played guitar and danced. In the 2007 musical *Sweeney Todd: The Demon Barber of Fleet Street*, Johnny sang and danced.

Sweeney Todd was originally a musical play. In the movie, Johnny acted alongside British actress Helena Bonham Carter.

Actors 101

Ryan Gosling (1980–)

Ryan was born on November 12, 1980, in London, Ontario, Canada. In 1993, he went to a *Mickey Mouse Club* (MMC) audition. Ryan beat 17,000 other children to win a spot on the show. For the next two years, he appeared on MMC. Following MMC, Ryan appeared on various television series, including *Young Hercules*. Movie roles soon followed. In 2002, he earned an **Independent Spirit Award** nomination for his portrayal of Danny in *The Believer*. After appearing in *The Notebook*, Ryan's picture was on magazines around the world. In 2007, Ryan was nominated for an Academy Award for his work in *Half Nelson*.

Brad Pitt (1963–)

Brad Pitt was born in Oklahoma, but raised in Missouri. He moved to Hollywood in the mid-1980s to become an actor. His career started with small guest roles on several television series, including *Growing Pains* and *Dallas*. In 1991, he was given a small, but important, part in the movie *Thelma & Louise* that launched his movie career. Since then, Brad has appeared in several blockbusters and has been nominated for four Academy Awards.

Angelina Jolie (1975–)

Angelina Jolie was born into an acting family. Her father is Academy Award winner Jon Voight, and her mother was French actress Marcheline Bertrand. Angelina began acting at an early age and quickly made a name for herself. Her breakout role in the 1998 television movie *Gia* won her a Golden Globe Award. The following year, she won an Academy Award for her role in the motion picture *Girl, Interrupted*. In recent years, Angelina has ventured beyond acting and is now equally known for helping less fortunate people all over the world.

Robert Downey Jr. (1965–)

Robert Downey Jr. was born in New York City to a show business family. His father, Robert, was a filmmaker, and his mother, Elsie, was an actress. By the time he was five years old, Robert was appearing in his father's films. After his parents divorced, Robert moved to Los Angeles with his father and quickly began acting in movies such as *Baby It's You* and *Weird Science*. By the late 1980s, he was getting roles in major motion pictures. In 1993, he was nominated for an Academy Award for his lead role in *Chaplin*. Most recently, Robert played the role of Iron Man in *The Avengers*, one of the most popular movies of 2012.

The Oscar

Every year, the movie industry gathers in Los Angeles for the Academy Awards. This ceremony is held to celebrate actors, directors, producers, and other industry workers who have excelled in recent works. Every winner at the ceremony receives a statuette called an Oscar. The Oscar statuette consists of a golden knight standing on a reel of film. He holds a sword in his hands. Each Oscar is 13.5 inches (34.3 centimeters) tall and weighs about 8.5 pounds (3.9 kilograms). However, it is more than its weight in gold to those who win it.

Influences

Johnny credits many people with influencing his acting career. For each new role, Johnny looks to his friends, his directors, well-known musicians, everyday people, and childhood memories. Johnny loves to observe people. He finds people fascinating. Even when they may seem to be leading ordinary lives, they are special to Johnny. He watches their behavior and listens to their speech patterns. He then uses them to create his characters.

Johnny thought of actress Angela Lansbury and her character in *Death on the Nile* for his role in *Sleepy Hollow*, in which the character of Ichabod Crane was transformed from a schoolteacher to a detective. He remembered the sense of honesty and virtue she brought to her character. He tried to bring those traits into his portrayal of Ichabod Crane. He modeled Captain Jack Sparrow in *Pirates of the Caribbean* after Rolling Stones guitarist Keith Richards. As a result, Captain Jack Sparrow has the character of a man who has experienced the rock star lifestyle.

Keith Richards has achieved success as part of the Rolling Stones and as a solo artist.

When he was researching his role in *Edward Scissorhands*, Johnny went back into movie history to the work of silent movie star Charlie Chaplin. Johnny watched many of Chaplin's films before filming began. He then, like the silent movie actor, tried to convey as much emotion as possible through Edward's facial expressions and body language.

THE DEPP FAMILY

Johnny has two children with his former partner, Vanessa Paradis. Their names are Lily-Rose Melody and John Christopher, or "Jack." When Johnny is not acting, he spends much of his time at home with his family.

Johnny met Vanessa on the set of his movie *The Ninth Gate*.

Overcoming Obstacles

It was not easy for Johnny to carve his unique path in the movie industry. He had to stay true to himself, even if it meant fewer jobs and less money. It took unwavering confidence and focus to turn down roles in **big budget movies** for parts in smaller films.

When Johnny won the part of Tommy Hanson in *21 Jump Street*, it looked as if Johnny was destined to have a typical leading man film career. Johnny did not want to be a big star. He wanted to be an actor. The role on the television show was so far from the career that he wanted that he decided not to renew his contract. To stay true to this goal, he decided to leave the show.

Johnny has always been attracted to characters more than fame. In the 1995 movie *Don Juan DeMarco*, Johnny worked with film legend Marlon Brando. Johnny played a young man who believed he was a character from a play written in the 1600s.

Director Tim Burton saw that Johnny was interested in taking risks and developing as an actor. He decided to cast him as the lead character in *Edward Scissorhands*. The two men soon established a solid friendship. Johnny's second movie with Tim, *Ed Wood*, came at a low period in Johnny's life. He was struggling with being a celebrity and the direction his career was taking. By focusing on work, Johnny was able to get his life back in focus. He won the **London Critics' Film Circle Award** for best actor for his portrayal of movie director Ed Wood.

■ Johnny and Tim Burton have a close friendship. Johnny has even referred to Tim as a brother.

Achievements and Successes

Johnny's commitment to acting has earned him several awards. Many of these have come from his work with Tim Burton. Following the release of *Edward Scissorhands*, Johnny was nominated for Best Performance by an actor in a Motion Picture-Comedy/Musical at the Golden Globes. He repeated this nomination with his second Tim Burton movie, *Ed Wood*.

The *Pirates of the Caribbean* movies have also brought Johnny much recognition. Johnny received Golden Globe nominations for Best Performance by an actor in a Motion Picture-Comedy/ Musical for both *The Curse of the Black Pearl* and its sequel, *Dead Man's Chest*. As well, television news network CNN called Johnny's Captain Jack one of the greatest comedy performances of the 21st century.

■ In 2011, Johnny won the People's Choice Award for Favorite Movie Actor. He was given the award for his work in *The Tourist* and Tim Burton's *Alice in Wonderland*.

In 2007, Johnny was back in a Tim Burton film, playing the lead role in a horror musical called *Sweeney Todd: The Demon Barber of Fleet Street*. The movie industry was impressed. Johnny won the Golden Globe for Best Actor in a Motion Picture-Comedy/Musical as well as the award for Best Villain at the MTV Movie awards. The role also earned Johnny an Academy Award nomination for Best Actor in a Leading Role.

HELPING OTHERS

Often, actors use their popularity to increase public awareness. They may bring attention to nonprofit organizations, environmental causes, or help fund special causes. Johnny has given much of his support to children's health care facilities, including the Children's Hospital Los Angeles and Ronald McDonald House. In 2006, he received the Courage to Care award. This award recognized Johnny's involvement with the Children's Hospital Los Angeles. Over the years, Johnny has helped raise funds for the Children's Hospice and Palliative Care Coalition. The organization works to improve care for children with life-threatening conditions and their families. To learn more about this charity, visit www.chpcc.org

Write a Biography

A person's life story can be the subject of a book. This kind of book is called a biography. Biographies describe the lives of remarkable people, such as those who have achieved great success or have done important things to help others. These people may be alive today, or they may have lived many years ago. Reading a biography can help you learn more about a remarkable person.

At school, you might be asked to write a biography. First, decide who you want to write about. You can choose a actor, such as Johnny Depp, or any other person. Then, find out if your library has any books about this person. Learn as much as you can about him or her. Write down the key events in this person's life. What was this person's childhood like? What has he or she accomplished? What are his or her goals? What makes this person special or unusual?

A concept web is a useful research tool. Read the questions in the following concept web. Answer the questions in your notebook. Your answers will help you write a biography.

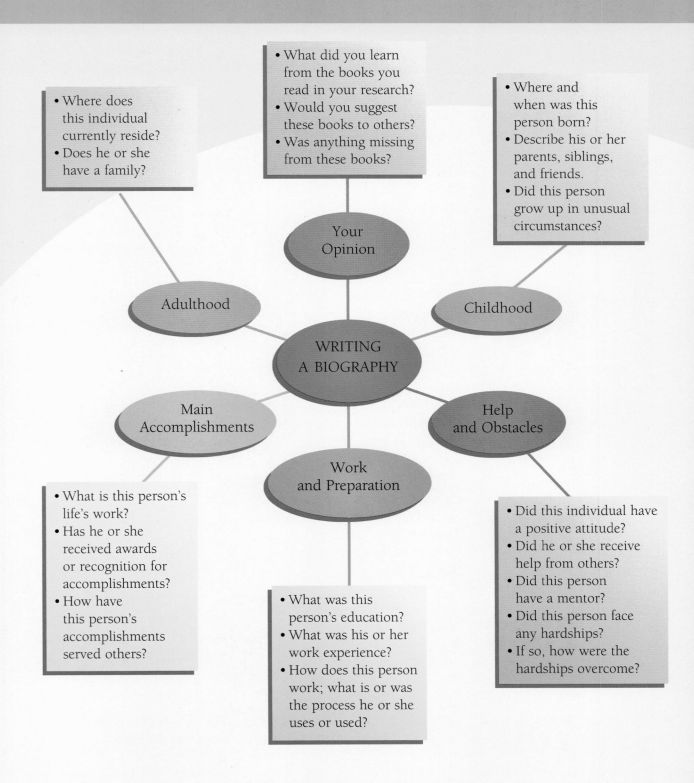

- What did you learn from the books you read in your research?
- Would you suggest these books to others?
- Was anything missing from these books?

- Where does this individual currently reside?
- Does he or she have a family?

- Where and when was this person born?
- Describe his or her parents, siblings, and friends.
- Did this person grow up in unusual circumstances?

Your Opinion

Adulthood

Childhood

WRITING A BIOGRAPHY

Main Accomplishments

Help and Obstacles

Work and Preparation

- What is this person's life's work?
- Has he or she received awards or recognition for accomplishments?
- How have this person's accomplishments served others?

- What was this person's education?
- What was his or her work experience?
- How does this person work; what is or was the process he or she uses or used?

- Did this individual have a positive attitude?
- Did he or she receive help from others?
- Did this person have a mentor?
- Did this person face any hardships?
- If so, how were the hardships overcome?

Timeline

YEAR	JOHNNY DEPP	WORLD EVENTS
1963	Johnny is born on June 9 in Owensboro, Kentucky.	The world's first multiplex movie theater opens in Kansas City, Missouri.
1983	Johnny moves to Los Angeles with his wife and bandmates.	More than 125 million people watch the last episode of the television comedy *M*A*S*H*.
1987	Johnny plays Officer Tom Hanson on a new television show called *21 Jump Street*.	*Platoon* wins the Academy Award for best picture.
1999	Johnny receives a star on the Hollywood Walk of Fame.	The Academy Awards take place on a Sunday for the first time.
2004	Johnny receives his first Academy Award nomination for his role as Captain Jack Sparrow in *Pirates of the Caribbean: The Curse of the Black Pearl.*	Film legend Marlon Brando dies on July 1 at the age of 80.
2008	Johnny wins Golden Globe for Best Performance by an actor in a Motion Picture-Musical/Comedy for *Sweeney Todd.*	Hollywood writers are on strike, causing problems for television shows and movies.
2010	Johnny is listed as the world's highest paid actor in the *Guinness Book of World Records.*	*The Hurt Locker* wins the Academy Award for Best Picture.

Key Words

Academy Award: an award by the Academy of Motion Picture Arts and Sciences for achievements in motion picture production and performance

animated: constructed in the form of a cartoon

big budget movies: films that are given major funding from movie studios

blockbuster: a movie that is a financial success

civil engineer: an engineer trained in the design and construction of public works, such as bridges or dams

diction: the choice and use of words and phrases in speech or writing

extra: someone who has a non-speaking role in a movie

Golden Globe: an award presented by the Hollywood Foreign Press Association recognizing excellence in film and television

Independent Spirit Award: an award recognizing achievements in independent filmmaking

leading man: an actor who plays the principal male role in a motion picture

London Critics' Film Circle Award: an award given by movie reviewers in the United Kingdom

nominated: placed on lists to be considered for an award

novice: a person new to a field or activity

opening acts: entertainers who perform before the featured act

recording contract: a legal agreement between a record company and a recording artist

scripts: documents containing the lines of characters in movies

set: a session of music that contains a certain number of songs

telemarketer: someone who sells products over the telephone

Index

Log on to www.av2books.com

AV² by Weigl brings you media enhanced books that support active learning. Go to www.av2books.com, and enter the special code found on page 2 of this book. You will gain access to enriched and enhanced content that supplements and complements this book. Content includes video, audio, web links, quizzes, a slide show, and activities.

Audio
Listen to sections of the book read aloud.

Video
Watch informative video clips.

Embedded Weblinks
Gain additional information for research.

Try This!
Complete activities and hands-on experiments.

WHAT'S ONLINE?

 Try This!

Complete an activity about your childhood.

Try this activity about key events.

Complete an activity about overcoming obstacles.

Write a biography.

Try this timeline activity.

 Embedded Weblinks

Learn more about Johnny Depp's life.

Learn more about Johnny Depp's achievements.

Check out this site about Johnny Depp.

Video

Watch a video about Johnny Depp

Check out another video about Johnny Depp.

EXTRA FEATURES

 Audio
Listen to sections of the book read aloud.

 Key Words
Study vocabulary, and complete a matching word activity.

 Slide Show
View images and captions, and prepare a presentation.

 Quizzes
Test your knowledge.

AV² was built to bridge the gap between print and digital. We encourage you to tell us what you like and what you want to see in the future.
Sign up to be an AV² Ambassador at www.av2books.com/ambassador.